People of
Ohio

Marcia Schonberg

Heinemann Library
Chicago, Illinois

**Library of Congress
Cataloging-in-Publication Data**
Schonberg, Marcia.
 People of Ohio / Marcia Schonberg.
   v. cm. -- (Heinemann state studies)
Includes bibliographical references and index.
Contents: Ohio's earliest residents -- Ohio's people --
Immigration to Ohio -- Those who came and stayed --
Ohio's achievers. ISBN 1-4034-0668-5 (HC) -- ISBN 1-
4034-2692-9 (PB)
1. Ohio--History--Juvenile literature. 2. Ohio--Popula-
tion--Juvenile literature. 3. Ethnology--Ohio--Juvenile lit-
erature. 4.Ohio--Biography--Juvenile literature. [1. Ohio-
-History. 2. Ohio--Biography.] I. Title. II. Series.
 F491.3.S368 2003
 305.8'009771--dc21
                                    2002154207

Acknowledgments
The author and publishers are grateful to the
following for permission to reproduce copyright
material:

Cover photographs: (top, L-R) Bettmann/Corbis,
Layne Kennedy/Corbis, Bettmann/Corbis,
Hulton-Deutsch Collection/Corbis; (main) Julian
O'Loughlin/Ohio State Fair

Title page (L-R) AFP/Corbis, Bettmann/Corbis, AP
Wide World Photos; contents page (L-R) courtesy
Heidi Hickey, Bettmann/Corbis, Corbis; pp. 7, 10,
19, 45 maps.com/Heinemann Library; p. 8 Richard
A. Cooke/Corbis; p. 11 Old World Auctions/
oldmaps.com; pp. 13, 18, 21B Ohio Historical
Society; p. 14 courtesy Heidi Hickey; p. 15 Jim
Baron/The Image Finders; p. 16 Philip Gould/
Corbis; p. 20 Amy Sancetta/AP Wide World Photos;
pp. 21T, 27B, 30, 31, 33, 41, 43, 44B Bettmann/
Corbis; p. 22 Catherine Karnow/Corbis; p. 23
courtesy Historical Shaker Museum; pp. 24, 25, 26,
27T Corbis; p. 28 AFP/Corbis; p. 34 Doug Mills/
AP Wide World Photos; p. 35 Reuters NewMedia
Inc./Corbis; p. 36 Stock Montage, Inc.; p. 37
Howard Jacqueline/Corbis SYGMA; pp. 38, 39 AP
Wide World Photos; p. 40 Hulton-Deutsch
Collection/Corbis; p. 42 Kurt Krieger/Corbis;
p. 44T Douglas Kirkland/Corbis

Photo research by Amor Montes de Oca

Every effort has been made to contact copyright
holders of any material reproduced in this book.
Any omissions will be rectified in subsequent
printings if notice is given to the publisher.

Some words are shown in bold, **like this.**
You can find out what they mean by looking
in the glossary.

Contents

Ohio's People

Ohio has earned several nicknames, thanks to the people who call the state home. Ohio is probably best known as the Mother of Presidents, but the Buckeye State is also home to many people who have made great contributions to our lives, including astronauts, inventors, authors, and more. The people of Ohio have made the state an interesting and **diverse** place to live and visit.

THE HEART OF AMERICA

Ohio became a state in 1803 and was settled by people from every state that already existed in the Union. It was the first state in what is now considered the Midwest of the United States and the people of Ohio reflect traditional Midwestern values. Family and neighborhood connections, hard work, and practical ideas are at the heart of Ohio's people.

OHIO'S CENSUS DATA

According to the 2000 U.S. **Census,** Ohio is the seventh largest state in population, with 11,416,018 residents. Ohio has seven cities of more than 100,000 people. Only California, Florida, and Texas have more cities of this size. The largest city in Ohio is Columbus, with a population of 711,470 people in the year 2000. Columbus's **metropolitan** area has over 1.5 million people.

Ohio's people represent many races and **ethnicities.** The 2000 census reported that 85 percent of Ohio's people were Caucasian and 11 percent were African American. This means that out of every 100 people in Ohio, 85 of them will be Caucasian and 11 will be African American. Other peoples, such as Asians, Hispanics, and Native Americans, make up a very small

Ohio's Demographics: 1990 vs. 2000

Navtive Hawaiian/ Other Pacific Islander
- 0%
- .01%

American Indian/ Alaska Native
- 0.002%
- 0.2%

Asian
- 0.007%
- 1.2%

Two or more races
- Not an option at time of 1990 census
- 1.4%

Some other race
- 0.005%
- 0.8%

African American
- 10.9%
- 11.5%

Caucasian
- 89%
- 85%

1990
2000

Source: U.S. Census Bureau, 2000

Ohio's people became more racially diverse between 1990 and 2000.

percentage of the population. When added all together, these groups of people total less than five percent of the people living in Ohio.

Ohio is among the nation's most **multicultural** states. Within each race of people, there are several ethnicities represented. Ohio has Irish, Amish, German, Polish, English, and several other groups of people spread throughout the state.

WHERE DO OHIO'S PEOPLE LIVE?

Northeast Ohio, near Cleveland and toward Ohio's border with Pennsylvania, is the most heavily populated area of the state. Northwestern Ohio is a **rural** area, with farmlands and many small villages

Reaching 100

In 2000, all 88 Ohio counties had at least one person older than 100. Central Ohio had 181 **centenarians,** including four in Franklin County who had reached 110 years of age.

Top Ten Ohio Cities by Population
1990 vs. 2000

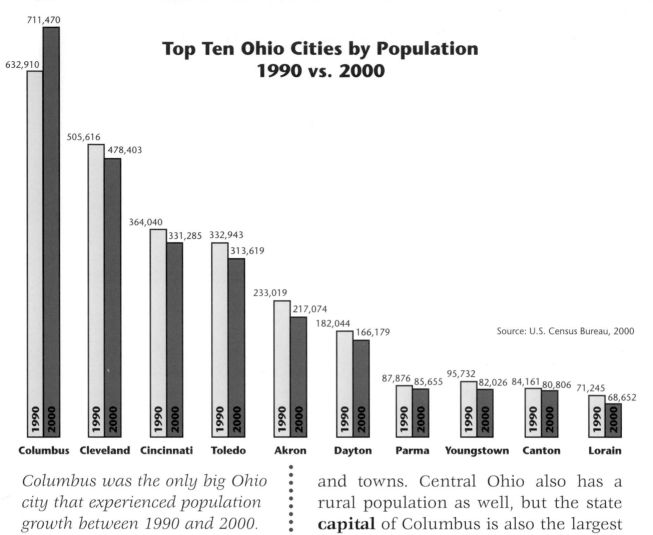

Source: U.S. Census Bureau, 2000

	Columbus	Cleveland	Cincinnati	Toledo	Akron	Dayton	Parma	Youngstown	Canton	Lorain
1990	632,910	505,616	364,040	332,943	233,019	182,044	87,876	95,732	84,161	71,245
2000	711,470	478,403	331,285	313,619	217,074	166,179	85,655	82,026	80,806	68,652

Columbus was the only big Ohio city that experienced population growth between 1990 and 2000.

and towns. Central Ohio also has a rural population as well, but the state **capital** of Columbus is also the largest **urban** area in the state. Southeastern Ohio has a widely-scattered population with only a few small **urban** centers, such as Marietta, Zanesville, and Chillicothe. The population in south-western Ohio is concentrated in the Miami Valley area. Dayton and Cincinnati are the most heavily-populated cities here.

About three out of every four people in Ohio live in urban areas. Ohio's ten biggest cities by population are Columbus, Cleveland, Cincinnati, Toledo, Akron, Dayton, Parma, Youngstown, Canton, and Lorain. However, most of Ohio's biggest cities lost population between 1990 and 2000 as more people moved to **suburban** areas.

Ohio has a total of 15 **metropolitan** areas. About two of every five people in Ohio live in the three

Ohio Population Change by County, 1990 vs. 2000

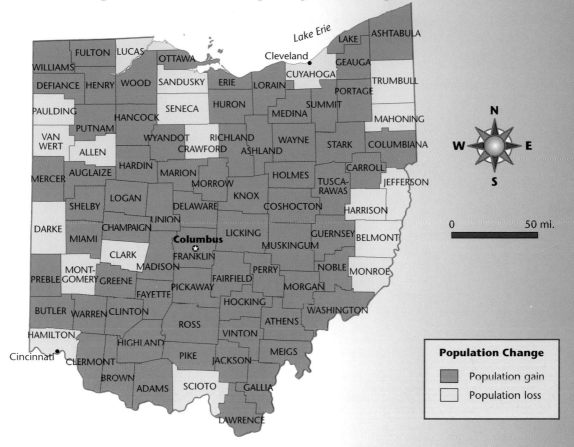

Population Change
- Population gain
- Population loss

largest metropolitan areas: Cincinnati, Columbus, and Cleveland. This includes not only the people who live in the city itself, but also those in the suburbs around it.

Ohio's county populations reflect how people move in and out of Ohio. Over the ten-year period between 1990 and 2000, most counties grew in population.

Five metropolitan areas in Ohio are partly in Ohio and partly in a neighboring state, such as Indiana, West Virginia, or Kentucky. These areas include Parkersburg-Marietta, Steubenville-Weirton, and Wheeling, all shared with West Virginia; Huntington-Ashland, shared with West Virginia and Kentucky; and Cincinnati, which is shared with Indiana and Kentucky.

Ohio's people have a variety of backgrounds and live in a range of communities. This **diversity** has helped Ohio achieve one more nickname, the Heartland.

Ohio's Earliest Residents

PALEO-INDIANS

The first people to arrive in the area that is now Ohio were **prehistoric** nomads, or wanderers. About 14,000 years ago, they crossed the land bridge of Beringia between Asia and Alaska. They were following the bears, mammoths, mastodons, and other animals that they hunted for food. When the animals became **extinct,** the hunters no longer had food, so they disappeared as well.

PREHISTORIC INDIANS

Ohio was home to many prehistoric peoples, including the Archaic Indians and the Moundbuilders—the Adena and the Hopewell Indians. They were called Mound-builders because of the mounds of earth they built where they lived. Their tribe names of Adena and Hopewell come from the places in Ohio where their tools, pottery, and mounds were found.

No one is exactly sure of the meaning of Serpent Mound, but it most likely symbolized some religious or mythical idea for its builders, the Adenas.

The Ft. Ancient people made their homes at the same site built earlier by the Hopewell Indians. They lived on the hilltop enclosure now called Ft. Ancient, near Lebanon in southeastern Ohio.

The Whittlesey people lived along Lake Erie and the Chagrin, Grand, and Cuyahoga Rivers about 1000 years ago. They built their ancient villages overlooking the rivers because the rivers provided easy access to transportation and food.

Native County Names

Although today there are no Native American **reservations** in the state of Ohio, the influence of the native peoples is still evident. Several counties in Ohio have names that come from Native American words.

Ashtabula	named after the Ashtabula River, meaning "fish river."
Auglaize	named after the Auglaize River, meaning "fallen timbers."
Coshocton	means "black bear town."
Cuyahoga	named after the Cuyahoga River, meaning "crooked."
Hocking	shortened from the word Hockhocking, meaning "bottled river."
Muskingdum	means "by the side of the river."
Pickaway	a version of the Native American word "piqua," meaning "man coming out of the ashes."
Portage	named after the Native American **portage** in the area.
Sandusky	a version of a Native American word meaning "cold water." In Wyandot and Huron languages, it is "Sa-un-dos-tee," meaning "water within water pools."
Mahoning	means "at the **licks.**"
Scioto	named for the Scioto River, meaning "deer."
Tuscarawas	named for the Tuscarawas River, meaning "open mouth."

The counties of Miami, Delaware, Wyandot, Ottawa, and Seneca are all named after the tribes that lived in those areas.

HISTORIC NATIVE AMERICANS

When the historic Native Americans arrived in the Ohio area in the 1600s, they came in search of new hunting grounds and a place to live after being pushed out of eastern settlements. The Iroquois, who hunted and traded furs for guns, beads, and tools, attempted to take over western lands. Six groups of Native Americans remained before being forced to move to **reservations** in Kansas or Oklahoma. These groups were the Ottawa, Wyandot, Mingo, Miami, Shawnee, and Delaware.

Today, about 24,000 Native Americans live in Ohio. They represent many different groups, including the Shawnees, Lumbees, Cherokee, and Miami. Several festivals are held in Ohio each year, including the Feast of the Flowering Moon in Chillicothe and the Great Mohican Indian Powwow in Loudonville.

Ohio's native peoples lived all over the state before settlers pushed them out.

Native Tribes of Ohio

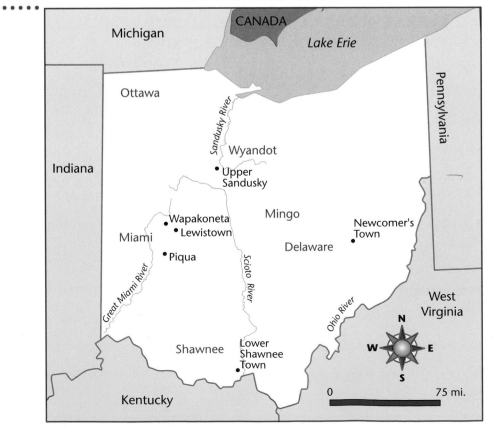

Settlement of Ohio

Before Ohio became a state in 1803, it was part of the Northwest Territory. There were few established settlements in this area until the the passage of the Land **Ordinances** of 1785 and 1786, and the Northwest Ordinance of 1787. These ordinances allowed people to buy land in the present-day Ohio area. People came from all over the country and the world to claim their land.

The area that became Ohio was in a good position for settlement of its land. Its southern boundary was the Ohio River, which became a major **thoroughfare** for **migrants** moving south and west. To the north were the Great Lakes, which became an extremely important westward passageway after the opening of the Erie **Canal** in 1825. There are also no natural barriers, such as mountains or deserts, to keep people from reaching the area. Many people who lived in the eastern United States, including in Connecticut, Pennsylvania, and New Jersey, moved westward to the Ohio area.

By the 1800s, people of several different **nationalities,**

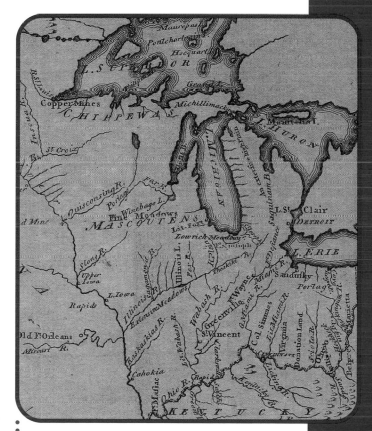

The Northwest Territory land eventually became the states of Ohio, Michigan, Indiana, and Wisconsin.

cultures, and religions had settled in Ohio. The first large group of **immigrants** came to Ohio before the Civil War (1861-1865). These people immigrated for many reasons. Some wanted to escape war and fighting in their homeland. Still others left their homelands to escape **famine.** Others could not find jobs in their countries to support their families. The United States offered better opportunities.

Many of the people who immigrated found jobs building transportation routes through Ohio, including roads and **canals.** After they completed the Ohio and Erie Canals, they then found work on the railroads. These new transportation routes helped to bring in even more people to Ohio.

Another big group of immigrants came to Ohio just after the Civil War. Most of these people came to work in the

The Western Reserve

Why did so many settlers from Connecticut come to Ohio? When the United States was formed, most of the former colonies had claims to unsettled lands in the West, where Ohio now was. All the states but Connecticut eventually gave these lands to the federal government. However, Connecticut wanted to use the land to repay their citizens who had lost everything during the Revolutionary War. The people who moved to Ohio called their special land here "New Connecticut." It consisted of what would later become the counties of Lorain, Cuyahoga, Lake, Ashtabula, Medina, Summit, Portage, Geauga, Trumbull, and the northern portion of Mahoning.

Workers used heavy equipment to dig through the layers of earth in order to create the Erie Canal.

manufacturing and mining **industries.** The U.S. government encouraged this **immigration** because more immigrants meant faster growth and more factory workers during the **Industrial Revolution.** New inventions, such as the steam locomotive, improved transportation. Industries led to the growth of many small towns in Ohio like Kent, and medium-size cities like Steubenville, Springfield, and Lima.

Immigrants were also attracted to the Ohio area because of the **fertile** soil. As the new-comers worked the land, Ohio became one of the top **agricultural** areas in the nation.

This flour and cotton mill was one of the industrial buildings located in Kent.

Ohio's Cultural Groups

At least 40 different languages, including English, Spanish, Italian, Polish, German, and Swedish, are spoken in Ohio. This is a reflection of the **diversity** of the state. African Americans, Native Americans, Germans, Italians, Irish, Poles, Hungarians, Latvians, Swedes, Czechs, and Norwegians are just some of the groups that live in Ohio. The state has more than 300,000 people who were not born in the United States. People come to live in Ohio for many different reasons. Each group that lives here contributes to the state in many ways.

Irish

Life was not always good in Ireland, especially in the 1800s. When the Irish heard that the United States had jobs and religious freedom, many of them boarded ships for the long, hard journey across the Atlantic Ocean.

About 500 Irish workers came to northeastern Ohio around 1817 to build the Ohio and Erie **Canals.** Thousands more came after Ireland's potato **famine** in 1848. The Irish from this period of **immigration** were mostly Roman **Catholic** and had a

Dancers perform traditional Irish dances at the Dublin Irish Festival each year.

great deal of influence on **parish** life in their communities. The Irish social life was also quite active, establishing many Irish societies and community celebrations. Celebrations of Irish-American life still happen today. Two of the biggest festivals are the Dublin Irish Festival held in Dublin, Ohio, and the Ohio Irish Festival held in Cleveland.

ITALIANS

For the Italians, very poor living conditions in their homeland villages in Italy sent them to the United States in search of a better life. Many of the Italian **immigrants** were stonecutters. They created many elaborate tombstones, built fancy churches, and installed beautiful marble and **mosaics** in Cleveland's public places. They printed their own newspaper and built the first Italian **Catholic** Church in Ohio in 1887. This church was the center for religious and social functions for the Italian community.

Some Italians came to Cleveland. The neighborhood they created, called Little Italy, is still one of the liveliest sections in Cleveland today. It has restaurants, bakeries, **ethnic** markets, and festivals. However, most Italians today live in the **suburbs.**

Little Italy is a popular place for visitors to Cleveland to see art or have an authentic Italian meal.

GERMANS

By 1850, nearly one half of Ohio's **immigrant** population came from various regions of Germany. In addition to settling alongside areas favored by the German immigrants in Pennsylvania, Ohio's German immigrants also settled in the Scioto and Miami Valleys and in Auglaize, Stark, and Tuscarawas Counties. Cincinnati, Cleveland, and other large Ohio cities also received German immigrants in great numbers.

The symbol of Cincinnati, the Tyler-Davidson Fountain, was created in Cincinnati's sister city, Munich, Germany.

By 1870, there were about 15,000 German immigrants in Cleveland. They represented the largest group of immigrants in Ohio at that time. German workers were eager to escape the fighting in Germany and come to the United States. Some of the immigrants were farmers or skilled craftspeople. They assisted with the building of the Ohio and Erie **Canals.** Some were jewelers, furniture builders, and cabinetmakers. Others built pianos and other musical instruments.

Cincinnati, on the Ohio River, already had a big German population by the time neighborhoods in Cleveland developed. German immigrants who came to Cincinnati to build the Miami and Erie Canal named their side

Columbus

Columbus, the state **capital,** is home to government employees and residents of varied backgrounds. Columbus did not develop strong **ethnic** neighborhoods like Cincinnati and Cleveland, except for German Village. Early German settlers lived in this area south of downtown. They were fine craftspeople and helped build the state **capitol** in 1812. As more German immigrants moved to Columbus, this neighborhood grew. By the mid-1800s, Columbus was one-third German. During World War I between the **Allies** and Germany, the United States supported the Allies. Anti-German feelings caused changes in this working class community. Streets with German names were changed to American names, and German books were destroyed. Today, the names have been changed back to the original ones. Small, neat, brick houses, beautiful gardens, wrought-iron gates, and brick streets and sidewalks make the neighborhood look like it did in the early days of German immigration.

of the canal "Over the Rhine," in honor of the major river in their homeland. Today, **descendants** of German immigrants celebrate their heritage at an annual festival called Oktoberfest. The Oktoberfest in Cincinnati is said to be the largest event of its kind in the United States, with over 500,000 people attending each year. Traditional dances, food, and music highlight the weekend.

German-Americans have greatly influenced the social, **cultural,** economic, and political life of southwestern Ohio. The Over-the-Rhine district, the Roebling suspension bridge, and Cincinnati's brewing tradition also provide evidence of the German influence on the city. Today, the German-American population continues to be strong in Ohio. Cincinnati, along with

The Parker House was home to John Parker, a former slave who settled in Ripley in the 1850s. Risking death or going to jail, he returned to the South to lead more than 1,000 slaves to freedom. The house has been designated a National Historic Landmark.

St. Louis, Missouri, and Milwaukee, Wisconsin, is part of the German Triangle, known for its high number of German-American residents. In the year 2000, nearly half of Cincinnati's population was of German **descent.**

AFRICAN AMERICANS

African Americans have been active throughout the history of Ohio. Prior to becoming a state, however, very few African Americans resided in Ohio. In 1800, only 337 African Americans lived in the area.

Ohio's first constitution, the Ohio Constitution of 1803, outlawed slavery. This was a requirement of the Northwest **Ordinance** of 1787. Because Ohio was a free state, Ohio's African Americans took an active role in the success of the Underground Railroad. The Underground Railroad was a network of homes or barns with hidden rooms and hiding places, secret tunnels, well-worn trails through thick woods, and "conductors" who led the runaway slaves to the next safe place. Ohio was directly between the slave states of the south and freedom in Canada. Many slaves passed through Ohio on their journeys. The African Americans provided food, shelter, and helped the runaway slaves to get to safety. The Underground Railroad helped pave the way for the establishment of several African-American settlements in Ohio, including Longtown and Palestine.

Many African Americans in Ohio were not allowed to attend white schools. This situation began to change when a law was passed in 1829. This law stated that African Americans could not attend public schools, but all school taxes paid by African American property owners had to be used to create schools for African-American children. In 1839, the Negro School Society of Columbus and the School Fund Institution of the Colored People of Ohio opened the first African-American school in Columbus.

Columbus has always been an important city for African Americans living in Ohio. African Americans settled in Columbus prior to 1850 because of its relative security and central location. They have been leaders of the city and involved in shaping its history throughout the 20th century. Today, Columbus is a popular place for African Americans to call home.

AMISH

Ohio has the largest population of Amish in the world. Their religion is called Anabaptist, which means "to be baptized again." The Amish left their homes in Switzerland and Germany in search of religious freedom. Not only did they find the freedom to practice their beliefs in Ohio, but Ohio's rolling hills also reminded them of the geography and landforms of their homelands. Most of the Amish population settled in Tuscarawas, Wayne, Holmes, Stark, and Coshocton Counties. There is also a smaller Amish community in Geauga County.

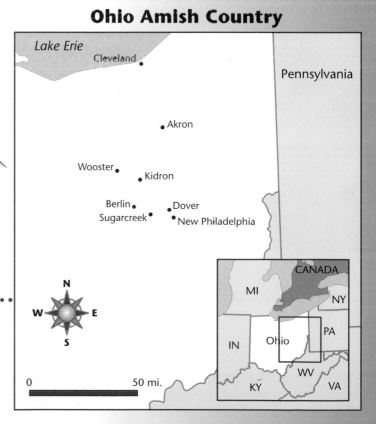

The Amish Country of Ohio is mostly located in the northeastern area of the state.

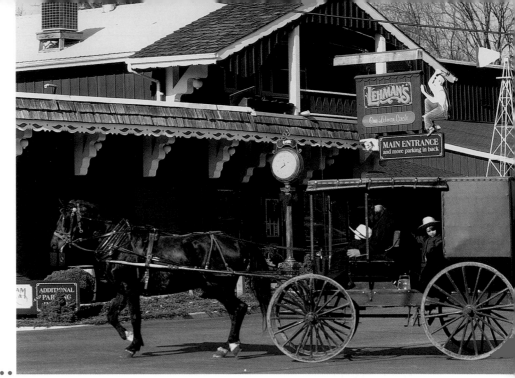

An Amish family drives their buggy past a hardware store in Kidron. Lehman's hardware store specializes in nonelectrical items and tries to promote a simple way of life.

Today, about 35,000 Amish people make their home in Ohio. Their first love is farming, but population growth means less land is available for farms. Many Amish people have gone to work in nearby factories or have home businesses, making furniture and handcrafts such as quilts, dolls, baskets, and baked goods.

The Amish way of life has changed very little since their arrival in Ohio. One of their main religious requirements is to live in their own communities, separate from the mainstream **culture.** However, tourism is a major **industry** for the Amish. Flocks of "English," the term they use to describe outsiders, visit and shop every weekend. The Amish sell **surplus** goods they have grown on their farms or have made by hand. There are even Amish restaurants for visitors to experience Amish-style cooking.

JEWS

By the 1870s, Jews from Europe began coming to the United States. They fled religious **persecution** in Russia and poor living conditions in Germany and other countries. In the eastern states, where the greatest numbers of Jewish people lived, it was easy to practice their religion. When they came to Ohio and other states in the Midwest, they built **synagogues.** However, it was difficult to fit into the American lifestyle in smaller cities. In 1873, a Jewish religious leader in Cincinnati, Rabbi Isaac Mayer Wise, developed Reform **Judaism,** a type of Judaism that was less restrictive than the earlier conservative and orthodox branches.

Rabbi Wise created the first school in the United States to train rabbis in Reform Judaism.

GERMAN SEPARATISTS

Two groups, the German Separatists and the English Shakers, set up communities in Ohio in the 1800s that no longer exist today. In 1817, the Separatists established a community in Zoar under the leadership of their founder, Joseph Bimeler. They helped visitors and strangers who came to their village, but their main goal was to work together to serve all of the needs of the community. They farmed, cooked, and educated the children as a community, owning nothing individually.

The Zoarite community never had more than 200 people. Even today, the community of Zoar, Ohio, has approximately 180 residents.

In 1827, the Zoarites were contracted to dig seven miles of the Ohio-Erie **Canal,** which passed through their land. Their work was completed in 1828 for $22,867.35, allowing them to pay off their land **debt,** due in 1830. The canal opened the area for **commerce.** At one time, the Zoarites operated as many as four canal boats. By the mid 1800s, Zoar was well known, and many people came to see the little German town in the Ohio hills.

Today, a popular furniture style called Shaker style follows the Shakers' ideas of straight legs and smooth finishes.

The group began to dissolve after Bimeler's death in 1853, and the community broke apart in 1898. Each community member received land, a house, and some of the groups' possessions. Today, the area is a tourist attraction, and the Ohio Historical Society maintains many of the buildings as museums.

THE SHAKERS

The Shakers settled near Cleveland in Shaker Heights, in Union Village near Lebanon, in Watervliet, and in Whitewater in the southwestern part of the state. Their religion and lifestyle began in England by a woman known as Mother Ann Lee. Shakers were skilled farmers and craftspeople. Part of their religion involved shaking when they prayed, giving them their name.

The North Union colony, one of the last Shaker communities in Ohio, was also known as The Valley of God's Pleasure. It was established in 1822 by Ralph Russell, a Warrensville settler and land owner. This Shaker colony included many members of his family and more than 80 of his neighbors.

The Shaker Historical Museum in Shaker Heights has many artifacts from the Shaker people of Ohio.

By 1850, at the peak of their membership, about 300 Shakers maintained the buildings and mills, operated their schools, and produced a wide variety of fruit, vegetables, and dairy products in the North Union colony. They packaged seeds and herbs. They made woolen items, flat brooms, boxes, baskets, and furniture for their own use and for sale. Not only did they support themselves, but they also shared what they had with the needy of Cleveland. However, by 1889, their numbers had dropped. The colony of North Union was closed, and the remaining Shakers relocated to southern Ohio.

The Shakers lived in Ohio until the end of the 19th century, when they finally disbanded. Shakers did not have children to carry on their religion. They depended on people from the outside to join their group. When that did not happen, the community died away.

In 1905, the property that was owned by the Shakers was bought by two **entrepreneurs,** M.J. and O.P. Van Sweringen. They developed Shaker Village, now called Shaker Heights, as one of the most carefully planned **suburbs** in the United States. The Van Sweringens designed sixteen styles of homes, planted trees, and provided land for schools and churches. They also added to the lakes built by the Shakers and developed the Rapid Transit System to provide convenient commuting to Cleveland. Since that time, the city of Shaker Heights has maintained standards of excellence similar to that of the early Shaker community.

Mother of Presidents

Ohio is called the Mother of Presidents because seven United States presidents were born in Ohio, and one claimed Ohio as his home state.

William Henry Harrison (1773–1841). Harrison was born in Virginia, but settled in Ohio later in life. He became the first Ohioan to reach the White House in 1889, as the ninth president of the United States. He was the first president to have a slogan, which was "Tippecanoe and Tyler, too." It refers to his successful battle against Native Americans in their town of Tippecanoe, Indiana, and the name of his vice president, John Tyler. He was president for only one month, the shortest term of any U.S. president. He caught a cold that became pneumonia, a lung infection. He died soon after.

Ulysses S. Grant (1822–1885). Born in Point Pleasant, Ohio, Ulysses S. Grant was named commander of the Union troops by President Lincoln during the Civil War (1861–1865). Grant became a Civil War hero as the general-in-chief of the Union armies. In 1869, Grant was elected the eighteenth president of the United States. While he was president, the Fifteenth Amendment of the U.S. Constitution gave African

Ulysses S. Grant

Americans the right to vote, and Yellowstone became our first national park.

Rutherford B. Hayes (1822–1893). Rutherford Hayes, from Delaware, Ohio, was the next president of the United States after President Grant. Like Grant, Hayes also served in the Civil War. During his time in office, Hayes ended **Reconstruction** with the withdrawal of the last federal troops from the South. He also forbid all federal employees from taking part in political activities. Hayes and his wife, Lucy, began the tradition of the annual White House Easter Egg Hunt. The Hayes Presidential Library in Fremont, Ohio, was the first presidential library.

Rutherford B. Hayes

James Garfield (1831–1881). James Garfield followed President Hayes to the White House as the twentieth president in 1881. Garfield grew up on a farm east of Cleveland in Orange and worked his way through college. Like several presidents before him, he also served in the Civil War. Garfield became president of Hiram College, then a lawyer, and then a member of Congress from Ohio. He served in Congress for eighteen years. Soon after taking office as the U.S. president, Garfield was **assassinated.** He died about two months later. His monument is in Cleveland's Lakeview Cemetery. His home is nearby in Mentor, Ohio.

Benjamin Harrison (1833–1901). The 23rd president, Benjamin Harrison, was from North Bend, Ohio. He was the grandson of President William Henry Harrison. Benjamin Harrison, too, served in the Civil War. During his presidency, he passed the Sherman Silver Purchase

Act of 1890, which required that silver be used in federal coins. This nearly wiped out the U.S. Treasury of its gold because it had to pay for all the silver that was used. Harrison was also in favor of high **tariffs,** which placed high **import** prices to protect American businesses, but also created high prices on American-made goods. He also supported the landmark Sherman Antitrust Act, the first bill ever to attempt to limit the power of America's giant businesses.

William McKinley (1843–1901). William McKinley was born in Niles, Ohio, attended school in Poland, Ohio, and set up a law practice in Canton. McKinley served two terms as Ohio's governor (1892–1896) and became the 25th president in 1897. Like the others before him, he too fought in the Civil War. During his time in office, Hawaii was **annexed** and the Spanish-American War took place (1898–1901). President McKinley enjoyed wearing a red carnation in his lapel each day, thinking it brought him good luck.

The president was **assassinated** in Buffalo, New York, during the Pan-American Exposition, becoming the third president to be killed while in office. In his memory, the red carnation became the official state flower of Ohio.

William Howard Taft (1857–1930). William Taft, from Cincinnati, had a long government career. He served as a judge in the Ohio Superior Court, the U.S. Solicitor General, a U.S. Circuit Court judge, the governor of the Philippines, the secretary of war, the president of the United States, and chief justice of the United States Supreme Court. He is the only man in U.S. history to have

William Howard Taft

been both president and chief justice. When Taft was president, New Mexico and Arizona were both admitted to the Union. The Sixteenth Amendment was passed, allowing the government to collect taxes on income. Taft and his wife, Helen, were the first president and first lady to be buried in Arlington National Cemetery in Virginia.

Warren G. Harding (1865–1923). Warren Harding was from Caledonia, Ohio, now called Blooming Grove. He was the last of the Ohio presidents to serve in the 20th century. After graduating from college, he moved to Marion, became the publisher of the *Marion Star* newspaper, served Ohio as **lieutenant governor** (1904–1906) and U.S. senator (1915–1921), and was president of the United States (1921–1923). His election was the first time women were able to vote.

Warren G. Harding

Harding's nickname, "Wobbly Warren," referred to his habit of changing his mind instead of sticking with his decisions. He allowed his **cabinet** members to make the decisions for him. Harding died in 1923, before his term of office was over, and was buried in Marion.

Ohio's Female Candidate

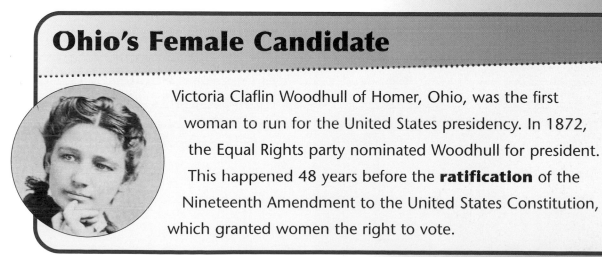

Victoria Claflin Woodhull of Homer, Ohio, was the first woman to run for the United States presidency. In 1872, the Equal Rights party nominated Woodhull for president. This happened 48 years before the **ratification** of the Nineteenth Amendment to the United States Constitution, which granted women the right to vote.

Mother of Astronauts

Ohio can also be called the Mother of U.S. Astronauts. Twenty-four astronauts came from Ohio. Nine, including Michael Good, who was in the Astronaut Class of 2000, are from Cleveland.

John H. Glenn, Jr. (1921–). The first American to **orbit** the Earth was John Glenn from New Concord. Glenn knew he wanted to fly at an early age. He got his chance during World War II, when he trained to become a pilot. After WWII, Glenn continued his pilot career. He flew missions in the Korean War and then became a famous test pilot before he volunteered to become one of the first American astronauts. His space mission aboard *Friendship 7* began February 7, 1962, when he lifted off from Cape Canaveral in Florida. During that mission, he orbited Earth three times in the 4 hours, 55 minutes, and 29 seconds that the spacecraft was in orbit.

John Glenn became a U.S. senator from Ohio in 1974 and served four terms, retiring in 1999. But his astronaut days were not over. In 1998, he boarded a spacecraft, *Discovery*, once again. At 77 years old, Glenn set another record as the oldest astronaut in the world.

John Glenn

Ohio's Astronauts and their Missions

Astronaut	Birth	Hometown	Mission(s)
Neil Armstrong	1930–	Wapakoneta	*Gemini 8, Apollo 11*
Charles Bassett II	1931–1966	Dayton	*Gemini 6A, Gemini 7*
Kenneth Cameron	1949–	Cleveland	STS-37, STS-56, STS-74
Nancy Currie	1958–	Troy	STS-57, STS-70, STS-88, STS-109
Donn Eisele	1930–1987	Columbus	*Apollo 7*
Michael Foreman	1957–	Wadsworth	In Training
Michael Gernhardt	1956–	Mansfield	STS-69, STS-83, STS-94, STS-104
John Glenn	1921–	New Concord	*Mercury-Atlas 6,* STS-95
Michael Good	1962–	Broadview Heights	In Training
Gregory Harbaugh	1956–	Willoughby	STS-39, STS-54, STS-71, STS-82
Karl Henize	1926–1993	Cincinnati	STS-51F
Thomas Hennen	1952–	Columbus	STS-44
Terence Henricks	1952–	Woodville	STS-44, STS-55, STS-70, STS-78
James Lovell	1928–	Cleveland	*Gemini 7, Gemini 12 Apollo 8, Apollo 13*
David Low	1956–	Cleveland	STS-32, STS-43, STS-57
Robert Overmyer	1936–1996	Westlake	STS-5, STS-51B
Ronald Parise	1951–	Warren	STS-35, STS-61
Judith Resnick	1949–1986	Akron	STS-41D, STS-51L
Ronald Sega	1952–	Cleveland	STS-60, STS-76
Robert Springer	1942–	Ashland	STS-29, STS-38
Donald Thomas	1955–	Cleveland	STS-65, STS-70, STS-94
Carl Walz	1955–	Cleveland	STS-51, STS-65, STS-79, STS-108
Mary Weber	1962–	Bedford Heights	STS-70, STS-101
Sunita Williams	1965–	Euclid	In Training

The Neil Armstrong Space Museum is located in Armstrong's hometown of Wapakoneta, Ohio.

Neil Armstrong (1930–). As a young boy of six, Neil Armstrong experienced his first airplane trip, sparking his interest in **aviation.** He built model airplanes and made a wind tunnel in his basement. Armstrong earned his pilot's license on his sixteenth birthday, even before he could drive a car. He served in the Korean War, flying 78 combat missions and winning three medals. Though Armstrong was on the backup crew of many previous flights, his first space flight occurred in 1966 aboard *Gemini 8*. During this flight, he and fellow astronaut David Scott successfully performed the first docking between two space vehicles.

Armstrong's most famous space mission occurred on July 21,1969, when the *Apollo 11* landed on the moon. People around the world watched Armstrong on television as he walked down the spacecraft steps and became the first person to walk on the moon. The words he spoke at that moment are historic: "That's one small step for a man, one giant leap for mankind."

James Lovell Jr. (1928–). James Lovell was born in Cleveland, Ohio. He served in the United States Navy and was selected for the National Aeronautics and Space Administration (NASA) space travel program in 1962. With Frank Borman, he made a record-breaking flight of 330 hours, 35 minutes in the 1965 *Gemini 7* mission. This mission was part of the first successful space link up between two ships. He and Edwin Aldrin **orbited** Earth in *Gemini 12* in 1966. In 1968, with Borman and William Anders, Lovell made the first manned flight around the moon in *Apollo 8*. Lovell was the commander of the space flight *Apollo 13* in 1970, which nearly ended in disaster when the oxygen and power systems in the ship failed after an explosion.

Working with fellow crew members Fred W. Haise and John L. Swigert Jr., Lovell guided the ship safely home. Lovell retired from the Navy and the space program in 1973.

Judith Resnick (1949–1986). Dr. Judith Resnick was born in Akron, Ohio. She was selected as an astronaut candidate by NASA in January 1978. After completing her training in 1979, Resnick worked on a number of projects for NASA before being a crew member on the first flight of the *Discovery* in 1984. On January 28, 1986, Resnick was a crew member on the space shuttle *Challenger*. Tragically, this shuttle exploded seconds after launch, killing all crew members aboard.

Judith Resnick

Nancy Currie (1958–). Dr. Currie was born in Wilmington, Delaware, but considers Troy, Ohio, her home. Currie served in the United States Army for over twenty years before coming to NASA in 1987 as a flight simulation engineer. She became an astronaut in 1990 and has flown on four missions: STS-57 *Endeavour* (June 21 to July 1, 1993), STS-70 *Discovery* (July 13–22, 1995), STS-88 *Endeavour* (December 4–15, 1998), and STS-109 *Columbia* (March 1–12, 2002).

Carl Walz (1955–). In 2001, Cleveland native Carl Walz spent six months in the International Space Station. Walz was a part of the *Expedition 4* crew that traveled to the space station aboard *Endeavour*. During their stay aboard the space station, they conducted and monitored experiments, and took several space walks. During his free time, Walz played a small musical keyboard and a guitar. He returned to Earth on June 5, 2002, breaking the U.S. space flight **endurance** record. Walz also holds the U.S. record for most **cumulative** time in space with 231 days.

Mother of Inventors

Many great ideas and inventions are those of people from Ohio. Items we use everyday, such as telephones, lightbulbs, and airplanes, were invented by Ohio residents.

Thomas Edison (1847–1931). Born in Milan, Ohio, Edison only had three months of formal schooling, at the age of seven. In his lifetime, Edison **patented** 1,093 inventions. His major inventions were the electric light bulb, the phonograph, the motion-picture projector, automatic and multiplex telegraph, the carbon telephone transmitter, a stock ticker, and the alkaline storage battery. Many of his inventions were among the most useful and helpful items ever developed.

Granville Woods (1856–1910). Born in Columbus, Ohio, Woods worked as **machinist** and **blacksmith,** as well as a firefighter on the railroad. He then became a steam locomotive engineer. As a skilled inventor, his first patent was for an improved steam boiler furnace. He received several more patents during his lifetime, including those for an improved telephone transmitter, in December 1884, and for numerous electrical systems for railways. To research, manufacture, and market his electrical inventions, Woods founded an electric company in Cincinnati, Ohio, in 1880.

Wilbur (1867–1912) **and Orville Wright** (1871–1948). Wilbur Wright was born in Indiana, but he and his family moved to Dayton before his younger brother, Orville, and their sister, Katherine, were born. The

brothers were fascinated with learning to fly, playing with kites and a toy helicopter. They developed several glider planes before the *Flyer I*, a gasoline-powered plane. Orville's attempt to fly at Kitty Hawk, North Carolina, on December 17, 1901, lasted only 12 seconds. Wilbur's flight that day was in the air for 59 seconds. Their short flights changed transportation forever. The *Flyer I* is now at the National Air and Space Museum in Washington, D.C.

Wilbur and Orville Wright

Charles Kettering (1876–1958). Born near Loudonville, Ohio, Kettering co-founded Delco (Dayton Engineering Laboratories Company) in 1909. He helped create the Delco electric power-generating and light-generating unit for farmhouses. He also developed improved lighting and **ignition** systems and the first electric starter for automobiles.

Garrett Morgan (1875–1963). In 1916, Morgan rescued workers after an explosion in a tunnel under Lake Erie. He entered the gas-filled tunnel wearing a safety hood he had patented two years earlier. His safety hood was what eventually became the modern gas mask. In 1923, Morgan patented another safety invention—the automatic traffic signal.

Elisha Gray (1835–1901). Elisha Gray was one of the cofounders of the Western Electric Company in Barnesville, where he invented the telephone. Gray and Alexander Graham Bell got into a legal battle regarding the right to patent the first telephone, as both claimed to have invented it first. In the end, Bell was awarded the patent. However, Gray held about 70 patents for other types of communication equipment.

Elisha Gray

Ohio's Achievers

Bellows, George (1882–1925), artist. George Bellows attended Ohio State University and studied painting in New York City. His subjects included **immigrant** neighborhoods in New York City and prizefights. In 1909, Bellows became the youngest artist ever elected an associate member of the National Academy of Design.

Halle Berry

Berry, Halle (1968–), actor. Halle Berry is a popular actor who was born and raised in Cleveland. Berry was named after a downtown department store named Halle Brothers. As a teenager, Berry won many beauty pageants, including Miss Ohio Teen. She was the first African American selected to represent her country in the Miss World contest. In 2000, Berry was also the first African American to earn an Oscar for Best Actress.

Bombeck, Erma (1927–1996), writer. Bombeck grew up in Dayton, Ohio, and became a column writer for the *Kettering-Oakwood Times* in 1964. Her work was **syndicated** in 1988, and readers from all over the world enjoyed her humorous words about parenthood. She also published several popular books, and appeared for eleven years on the television show *Good Morning America*.

Bromfield, Louis (1896–1956), author. Louis Bromfield was raised on a farm near Mansfield, Ohio. He studied **agriculture** in college and learned many ways to make farming more successful. At the same time, he was also interested in writing. He began writing novels about the people and places around him. Bromfield won the **Pulitzer Prize** for his novel about Ohio, *Early Autumn*. His farm is now the Malabar Farm State Park and his home, called the Big House, is open for tours.

Brown, Paul (1908–1991), football coach. Paul Brown is from Norwalk, Ohio. Brown worked his way up from coaching a high school football team in Massillon to the college-level Ohio State Buckeyes. The NFL Cleveland Browns got their name from Brown, as he was the very popular first coach of the team. Brown coached the Browns until 1962, then coached the Cincinnati Bengals from 1968 to 1975. Brown is honored in the National Football Hall of Fame in Canton, Ohio.

Drew Carey

Carey, Drew (1958–) actor. Drew Carey was born in Cleveland. He began his successful career as a comedian in April 1986 at the Cleveland Comedy Club. One of his first big breaks was competing on *Star Search* in 1988. His career then took several paths before he achieved success as the star of his own television show, *the Drew Carey Show*. Carey is also producer and host of the popular show *Whose Line Is It Anyway?*

Cartwright, Nancy (1957–), actor. Nancy Cartwright is originally from Dayton. Cartwright's achievements as an actor include dozens of credits in television, film, and theater. She is recognized as one of the world's leading voice-actors, and has received numerous awards and recognitions for her performances, including an Emmy for her work as the voice of Bart Simpson of the television show, *The Simpsons*. Cartwright is also the voice of Chuckie from the cartoon show *Rugrats*.

Crile, George Washington (1864–1943), physician. Dr. Crile was born in Chili, Ohio. He was a well-known surgeon who made great advances in helping patients who were undergoing surgery. He cofounded the Cleveland Clinic, now a large health center, and was the first doctor to successfully use direct **blood transfusions.**

Dove, Rita (1952–), poet. Rita Dove was born in Akron, Ohio. She served as **poet laureate** of the United States and consultant to the Library of Congress from 1993 to 1995. Dove was the youngest person, as well as the first African American, to receive this highest official honor. She has also received numerous literary and academic honors, including the 1987 **Pulitzer Prize** in poetry.

Paul Laurence Dunbar

Dunbar, Paul Laurence (1872–1906), poet. Paul Laurence Dunbar became a well-known poet and author because of the books he wrote in the **dialect** of southern slaves. His poems explain some of the secret terms slaves used in their hymns and church services to signal an escape.

Fisher, Sarah (1980–), race car driver. Fisher started racing cars at age five in Columbus, Ohio. She has raced all her life, but her biggest accomplishment was racing in the Indianapolis 500 in 2000. Fisher was the youngest woman ever to drive in an Indy race. In 2002, she became the fastest woman ever at Indy with a four-lap qualifying average of more than 229 miles per hour.

Gable, Clark (1901–1960), actor. Clark Gable was born in Cadiz, Ohio. He starred in more than 50 movies during his lifetime, earning an Academy Award for his performance in *It Happened One Night*. His hometown holds a celebration on his birthday (February 1) every year to honor him.

Gish, Lillian (1893—1993), actor. Lillian Gish, whose real name was Lillian de Guiche, was born in Springfield, Ohio. She was a famous actress of the silent movies in the early 1920s. With the change from silent films to films with sound in the late 1920s and early 1930s, Lillian alternated between performing on film and the stage. She made over 100 films in her lifetime.

Gompers, Samuel (1850-1924), American labor leader. Samuel Gompers, a worker from Columbus, organized employees according to their trade or job and formed the first union, the American Federation of Labor (AFL). Together, members had more power to have their voice heard and make changes to their working conditions. Today, the organization is called the AFL-CIO.

Grey, (Pearl) Zane (1872–1939), author. Except for the year 1916, a book by Zane Grey was in the top ten on the best-seller list every year between 1915 and 1924. Grey wrote more than 80 books during his career, and is credited with helping to create the literary style known as the Western. Zane Grey's family also founded the town of Zanesville, Ohio.

Arsenio Hall

Hall, Arsenio (1956–), entertainer. Arsenio Hall comes from an inner-city neighborhood in Cleveland. As a boy, he dreamed of being a talk show host like his idol, Johnny Carson. In 1989, he got his own late-night television show, *The Arsenio Hall Show*. The National Association for the Advancement of Colored People (NAACP) has honored this entertainer for his work to help improve **civil rights.**

Hamilton, Virginia (1936–2002), author. Virginia Hamilton started her life in the small town of Yellow Springs, Ohio. During her career as a children's writer, Hamilton produced original folktales and retellings, novels, mysteries, fantasy books, and nonfiction. Common to all these works was African American experiences, history, and **culture.** Hamilton was honored with numerous awards for her writing, including the Regina Medal in 1990, the Hans Christian Andersen Medal in 1992, and the Laura Ingalls Wilder Award in 1995.

Hope, Bob (1923–), entertainer. Leslie Townes Hope, better known as Bob Hope, was born in England but moved to Cleveland with his parents at age four. He spent many years entertaining U.S. military troops stationed overseas. He received numerous awards for his **humanitarian** work, efforts that brought happiness to others. He also starred in American movies and Broadway plays.

Maya Lin

Lin, Maya (1959–), **architect** and sculptor. Maya Lin was born in Athens, Ohio. While Maya was a student at Yale University, she entered a contest to design the Vietnam Veterans Memorial in Washington, D.C. About 1,400 artists entered the contest. Many were famous, experienced architects and much older than Maya. She was only 21 years old when her design won. Her idea, a dark marble wall with every name of the soldiers who died during the Vietnam War or are missing in action, was dedicated in 1982. She now lives in New York City and designs public sculptures around the country. Another of her famous works is the **Civil Rights** Memorial in Montgomery, Alabama.

Martin, Dean (1917–1995), actor. Dean Martin was born in Steubenville, Ohio, and given the name Dino

Corcetti. He sang Italian tunes in Columbus and other Ohio cities before linking up with comedian Jerry Lewis. Their comedy act took off and the two appeared in sixteen movies. After Martin split from Lewis, his solo career continued with several more movies and two television shows.

McGuffey, William Holmes (1800–1873), educator. William McGuffey grew up in Youngstown, Ohio, but moved to Oxford, hoping to get a teaching job. He taught at several colleges and was the president of Ohio University and Cincinnati College. McGuffey supported the bill that opened Ohio's first public school system. He wrote six different schoolbooks for children called *McGuffey's Eclectic Readers*. His books sold more than 122 million copies and became the standard textbook used by children throughout the country from the late 1800s through the mid 1900s.

Morrison, Toni (1931–), author. Toni Morrison comes from Lorain, Ohio. She studied literature in college and is a professor at Princeton University in New Jersey. She won the 1987 **Pulitzer Prize** for fiction for her novel, *Beloved*, and the **Nobel Prize** for Literature in 1993.

Toni Morrison

Newman, Paul (1925–), actor, **philanthropist.** Newman was born in Shaker Heights, a **suburb** of Cleveland, Ohio. He was a successful movie actor, receiving eight Academy Award nominations for Best Actor. Newman won the Academy Award for Best Actor in 1987 for his role in *The Color of Money*. Today Newman focuses on his philanthropic interests. The profits from his Newman's Own line of salad dressings and other food items have supported causes ranging from The Hole in the Wall Gang Camp for terminally ill children, to the Scott Newman Foundation for drug and alcohol abuse education, to **drought** relief in Africa.

Nicklaus, Jack (1940–), athlete. Jack Nicklaus, born in Columbus, began winning golf tournaments when he was just ten years old. While a student at Ohio State University, he won the U.S. **Amateur** Championship in 1959 and 1961. His golfing career spans more than 50 years, including winning a total of 100 national and international tournaments, 18 of them major championships.

Oakley, Annie (1860–1926), sharpshooter. Annie Oakley grew up in **rural** Greenville. She practiced shooting in the woods near her house. Oakley entered shooting contests, and when she convinced other sharpshooters of her talents, she decided to go on the road with the Buffalo Bill show, entertaining people across the United States and Europe. She amazed people with her ability to shoot so accurately.

Owens, Jesse (1913–1980), athlete. Owens, whose full name was James Cleveland Owens, moved to Cleveland when he was eight years old. Owens was an American track-and-field athlete who set a world record in the running broad jump (also called long jump). That record stood for 25 years. He also won four gold medals at the 1936 Olympic Games in Berlin.

Annie Oakley

Parker, John (1827–1900), businessperson, **abolitionist,** and freed slave. A slave as a young child, Parker understood the terrible life of slaves. He bought his own freedom as a teenager, working in an iron **foundry.** As an adult, Parker led an estimated 1,000 slaves to freedom over the Ohio border. In 1854, he settled in the town of Ripley. He was one of the first Ohio African Americans to own his own business, opening the Ripley Foundry and Machine Company. Parker received a **patent** for a screw for tobacco presses. He was also one of the few slaves to write a book about his slave experience. It is called *His Promised Land: The Autobiography of John P. Parker, Former Slave and Conductor on the Underground Railroad.*

Rockefeller, John D. (1839–1937), **industrialist** and **philanthropist.** John D. Rockefeller from Cleveland became Ohio's first millionaire after learning how to **standardize** the quality of petroleum oil. His company was called the Standard Oil Company. Rockefeller used his wealth to generously donate to many causes, giving more than $500 million during his lifetime.

John Rockefeller

Rose, Pete (1942–), athlete. Pete Rose grew up in Cincinnati, where a street bears his name. He played for the Cincinnati Reds and Philadelphia Phillies. By the time he retired as a player in 1986, Rose had a record career total of 4,256 hits. His other records included most games played—3,562; most times at bat—14,053; and most seasons with 200 hits or more—10. Rose then went on to manage the Reds. His talents should have earned him a spot in the Baseball Hall of Fame, but he was banned from baseball when he was accused of gambling on the games.

Steven Spielberg

Spielberg, Steven (1946–), director and producer. Steven Spielberg, born in Cincinnati, has a long list of impressive films to his credit. By the time he turned thirteen, he had already won a prize for a 40-minute film called *Escape to Nowhere.* Before hitting it big in the movies, Spielberg directed television programs and TV movies. *Jaws* was the movie hit that set him on the road to success. Then came movies like *Close Encounters of the Third Kind, Raiders of the Lost Ark, Indiana Jones and the Temple of Doom, E.T. The Extra-Terrestrial,* and *Jurassic Park. Schindler's List, Amistad,* and *Saving Private Ryan* have also brought Spielberg much attention. He writes many of the screenplays and has won many awards for his movies, including two Academy Awards for Best Director.

Steinem, Gloria (1934–), political **activist.** Gloria Steinem, a leader of the feminist movement in the late 20th century, was born in Toledo. Steinem wanted women to be treated equal to men. She began to work for women's rights. She graduated from Smith College with honors and found work as a **journalist.** Her writing career took many directions, including starting the magazine *Ms.* She spoke at the National Conference for Women in 1977. It was the first national meeting for women's rights and modern causes. She was **inducted** into the National Women's Hall of Fame in Seneca Falls, New York, in 1993.

Stine, R. L. (1943–), author. Robert Lawrence Stine was born in Columbus, Ohio, and grew up in the **suburb** of Bexley. His writing career began when he was nine years old, writing short stories, joke books, and comic books for his friends. Today he is the best selling children's author in history. He has devoted his adult life to getting children to enjoy reading and involving them in the fun and creativity of writing.

Stowe, Harriet Beecher (1811–1896), author. Stowe moved to Cincinnati with her family when she was 21 years old. In 1852, her book, *Uncle Tom's Cabin*, was published. With its descriptions of suffering and **oppression,** this book angered Northerners against slavery. It became a force in bringing about the American Civil War between the northern and the southern states. The book has been translated into more than 20 languages and presented countless times on the stage and in movies.

Tecumseh (ca. 1768–1813), Native American chief. Tecumseh grew up to be one of the greatest leaders in Native American history. He spent his life trying to unite tribes throughout the Ohio region and far beyond. He believed that the land belonged to everyone, and that Native Americans should be able to remain on the land. However, the European settlers and colonists moved farther west, crowding his people from their space. He refused to sign the Treaty of Greenville, but obeyed its rules. He fled to Canada during the War of 1812 and sided with the British, rather than give in to the settlers. He was killed in the Battle of Thames.

Tecumseh

Thurber, James (1894–1961), writer and cartoonist. James Thurber grew up in Columbus and attended Ohio State University. He held several newspaper jobs before going to New York City in 1926. Thurber was a reporter first for the *Evening Post*, then was the managing editor and staff writer for *The New Yorker* magazine. He published many cartoons and illustrations in the magazine as well.

Ted Turner

Turner, Ted (1938–), **entrepreneur.** Born Robert Edward Turner III in Cincinnati, Ohio, Ted Turner is one of the richest people in the United States. Turner started by selling rental space on billboards through his family's outdoor advertising business. He took over the company in 1963 and purchased one of Atlanta's local television stations seven years later. He then formed the Turner Broadcasting System (TBS). In 1976, Turner pioneered the "superstation" concept when he arranged to transmit the WTBS signal to cable systems around the country. Turner is also well-known as the owner of the Atlanta Hawks hockey team and Atlanta Braves baseball team, and for establishing the Cable News Network (CNN).

Young, Cy (1867–1955), athlete. Cy Young was the nickname of Denton True Young from Gilmore, Ohio. Young played baseball for the Cleveland Spiders from 1890 to 1898, the St. Louis Cardinals from 1899 to 1900, the Boston Red Sox from 1901 to 1908, the Cleveland Indians from 1909 to 1911, and the Boston Braves in 1911. He pitched 750 complete games and 7,356 innings, including a stretch of 23 hitless innings in a row in 1904. He recorded 76 shutouts and three no-hit, no-run games, including modern baseball's first perfect game, on May 5, 1904. Elected to the Baseball Hall of Fame in 1937, he is also honored by the Cy Young award, given each year to the best major league pitcher.

Cy Young

Map of Ohio

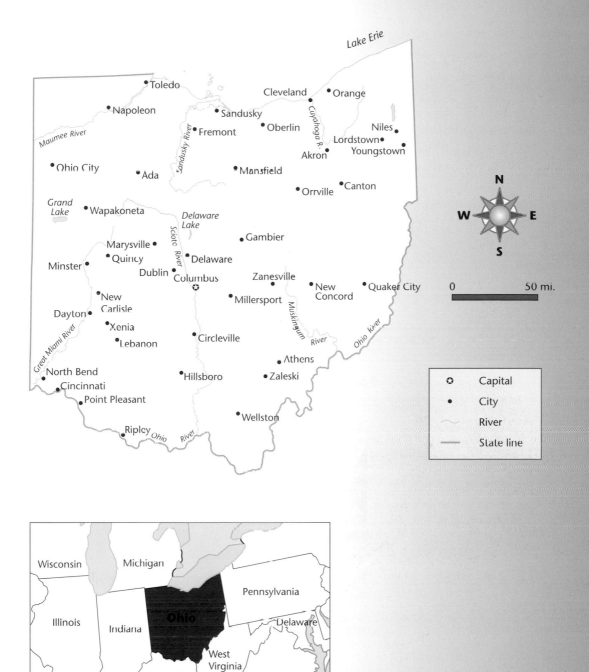

Glossary

abolitionist person who wanted to ban slavery

activist someone who publicly supports a cause

agricultural having to do with raising crops and farm animals

Allies nations that were against Germany and Italy in World War I

amateur person who takes part in sports for pleasure and not pay

annex add something to something else so the piece becomes part of the whole

architect person who designs buildings and gives advice on their construction

assassinate murder of an important person by surprise attack

aviation having to do with aircraft

blacksmith person who makes things out of iron by heating and hammering it

blood transfusion transfer blood into a person's body

cabinet group of persons who act as advisors to the president

canal artificial waterway for boats

capital location of a government

capitol building in which the legislature meets

Catholic member of the Roman Catholic Church

census annual count and gathering of information about a population

centenarian person 100 or more years old

civil rights rights of personal liberty guaranteed by the U.S. Constitution

commerce buying and selling goods

culture ideas, skills, arts, and a way of life of a certain people at a certain time

cumulative length in time without a break

debt owing money

descendant/descent to be born of

dialect form of language belonging to a certain region

diverse/diversity having variety

drought time of little or no rain

endurance ability to put up with strain, suffering, or hardship

entrepreneur person who starts a new business

ethnic/ethnicities belonging to a group with a particular culture

extinct no longer living

famine time when food is scarce and people are starving

fertile bearing crops or vegetation in abundance

foundry building or factory where metals are cast

humanitarian person devoted to and working for the health and happiness of other people

ignition process or means of setting a fuel mixture on fire

immigrant/immigration act of or person moving to another country to settle

import bring something into a country

inducted placed in office

Industrial Revolution period during the late 1800s and early 1900s when manufacturing developed in the United States

industrialist person engaged in the management of a group of businesses

industry group of businesses that offer a similar product or service

journalist someone in the business of collecting and editing news for the media

Judaism religion developed among ancient Hebrews that stressed belief in one god and faithfulness to the moral laws of the Old Testament

lick natural salt deposit

lieutenant governor second-in-command of a state, after the governor

machinist person who makes or works with machines

metropolitan area surrounding a large city

migrant person who moves from one place to another without a real destination

mosaic decoration on a surface made by setting small pieces of glass or stone of different colors into another material to make a pattern

multicultural made up of several different cultures

nationality group of people having a common history, tradition, culture, or language

Nobel Prize award given each year to someone who has excelled in helping others

oppression cruel or unjust use of power or authority

orbit path taken by one body circling around another body

ordinance law or regulation specific to a town or city

parish members of a church community

patent protect by a document that gives the inventor of something the only right to make, use, and sell the invention for a certain number of years

persecution continual treatment in a way meant to be cruel

philanthropist person who gives generously to help other people

poet laureate official poet of a state or country

portage carrying of boats or goods overland from one body of water to another

prehistoric from the time before history was written

Pulitzer Prize award given in the United States in several fields, including literature, journalism, and education

ratification given legal approval

Reconstruction period during and after the American Civil War in which attempts were made to solve the political, social, and economic problems arising from the readmission to the Union of the eleven Confederate states that had broken away at or before the outbreak of war

reservation public land set aside for use by Native Americans

rural of, or relating to, the country, country people, or country life

standardize make all alike

suburb city or town just outside a larger city; suburban means having to do with a suburb

surplus amount left over beyond what is needed

synagogue Jewish house of worship

syndicated sold for publication in many newspapers or television stations

tariff list of taxes placed by a government on goods coming into a country

thoroughfare main road

urban relating to the city

More Books to Read

Brown, Dottie. *Ohio (Hello USA)*. Minneapolis: Lerner Publications Company, 2001.

Marsh, Carole. *Ohio: The Ohio Experience*. Peachtree City, Ga.: Gallopade Publishing Group, 2000.

Schonberg, Marcia. *B is for Buckeye: An Ohio Alphabet*. Chelsea, Mich.: Sleeping Bear Press, 2000.

Index

About the Author

Marcia Schonberg is a lifelong resident of Ohio. She writes regularly for daily newspapers and regional and national magazines. Her list of books includes the children's book *B is for Buckeye*. A graduate of Ohio State University, Schonberg now makes her home in Lexington with her husband Bill.